Guest Blogging Master Class

Your Step by Step Guide to Getting More
Traffic, Email Subscribers, and Sales

By Mike Fishbein

www.mfishbein.com

Table of Contents

Introduction

So, you've got a website...now you just need traffic and customers. After all, what's the point of having a beautiful site with great content if no one is looking at it? Customer acquisition is one of the biggest challenges of building an online business of any kind. Building websites has become cheaper and easier, but getting customers is as hard as ever.

Getting people to visit your site is the first step in the customer acquisition process. And doing so is much different than it used to be.

Traditional marketing and advertising is broken. Traditional advertising methods such as billboards, TV and radio advertising, snail mail marketing, and cold calling are expensive, hard to measure, and inefficiently targeted. As a result, they tend to be ineffective as well..

In addition, people usually find them really annoying. How many times do you switch to a different TV channel when a commercial is running? You know an industry is in trouble when people are actively paying for services so they don't have to see ads pop up. . People don't get sold to anymore, they buy. Annoying people by shoving products in their face is not a good way to get them to buy something! Nowadays, consumer buying behavior is different.

Enter content marketing, a more efficient and effective way to attract, engage, and acquire customers.

What exactly is content marketing? Let's clear this up so we're on the same page for the rest of the book. First, we will provide a rather "dense" definition of content marketing and then we'll break down each component of it.

Content marketing is a strategy for attracting, engaging, and acquiring customers. It entails creating and/or curating relevant and valuable content. Valuable content means you are helping and entertaining your readers.

Content marketing occurs in five phases. In the first phase, you will determine who your customers are. Second, you will figure out where they are in order to acquire new customers. Third, you will create content that draws them in. Fourth, you will engage with them, which is an important step that leads you right to the final and most important step, acquiring them as customers.

This book focuses primarily on getting in front of your customers and how to attract and engage with them. Guest blogging supplements these steps perfectly, as it will bring you to exactly where your customers/audience already are while providing them value.

Why Content Marketing Rocks

Why is content marketing such a great customer acquisition strategy? There are many reasons.

First, it allows you to reach these massive audiences of people and potential customers. You can build rapport and engage with them on a personal level. From the perspective of your potential customers, you will become an authority in your given space.

In addition, it's often a low cost acquisition strategy (though it does require time) and it is efficient since it is highly targeted and pays dividends over time. For example, when I wrote "How to Write a Book in 10 Days", I wrote a guest post on Convince and Convert because I knew the readers were mostly marketers interested in creating more content. We'll get into case studies later on in the book.

Content marketing is also quite sustainable and automated. If done well, it can maintain itself and continually acquire customers over time without work beyond your initial launch. Nothing like free, automated traffic and leads!

Guest Blogging: What this book covers

Do you ever feel like blogging on your own site is like farting in the wind? Have you been blogging for months, but still not ranking on Google for your target search terms?

Google has grown smarter, so the quick hacks don't really work anymore.

Ever tried reaching out to journalists to get press coverage only to hear crickets?

Most businesses will never get press coverage. Most journalists delete most of the pitch emails they get before even reading them.

Maybe you've tried spending money on ads, a fancy public relations agency, or sales/business development.

The reality is, getting customers is hard when everyone is a media company.

Enter: Guest blogging

Throughout this book you'll learn how to pitch editors and get your blog posts published on top sites. You'll also learn how to build your email list, get backlinks, boost your SEO, and find the best guest blogging opportunities for your business.

About the Author

I'm Mike. I do content marketing. I'm the author of multiple books on entrepreneurship and marketing. I've advised both startups and Fortune 500 companies on content marketing and product management. I've had my writing featured on top sites like Entrepreneur, Huffington Post and The Next Web. Previously I worked at a tech startup in New York doing marketing and product management.

I'm passionate about helping people start and grow businesses, and creating content that people love.

Not only do I produce content to market products and services but I actually sell the content itself, providing multiple passive income streams. In order to create content that is so valuable that people will even pay significant amounts of money for it, as you can imagine, it has to truly solve a problem and be perceived as unique and extremely valuable. Below are the strategies and tactics I've used to create content that is valuable enough that people pay for it.

You can check out my blog at mfishbein.com and my books at mfishbein.com/amazon.

Bonus content

If you want to achieve marketing success, you'll need a few more things beyond what's covered in this book. You'll need to find the time to create content, make sure the content provides value to your audience, and then tap into even more networks to further increase your traffic.

Fortunately, since you've purchased this book, I'm going to provide you with three *free* ebooks that cover these very topics! With this book, along with the three below, I'm confident you'll be well on your way to content marketing success.

How to Find Time to Write Great Content

The hardest parts about writing is getting started. In this book, I show you how to overcome writer's block and get in the zone. I'll teach you practical tips that will help you write great content for the rest of your life.

http://mfishbein.com/find-time-write/

Blog Topics That Drive Traffic and Convert Leads

Want free, automated traffic and leads? It's not as difficult as you may think. This book will help you reach massive audiences, build rapport with them, and boost your authority through your blog. And, you won't need to spend lots of money! If you want more traffic and more email subscribers, then this book is for you.

http://mfishbein.com/awesome-content/

More Content Networks

So you've got an awesome product or website…now you just need visitors! Customer acquisition is one of the biggest challenges of building an online business of any kind. This book shows you how to drive traffic to your site using content marketing. You'll learn how to use different platforms to reach new audiences. Give this book a read and get more traffic with content.

http://mfishbein.com/content-marketing-ebook/

Chapter 1

How Guest Blogging Can Help You Win

It's hard to start a blog from scratch. Technology has made it easier than ever before to start a blog. Suddenly everyone is a media company. As a result, it's harder than ever to rank on Google.

Why would you want to rank high on google? Two words: traffic and customers.

Because it is important to obtain customers in any business, and it can be difficult to start a blog, many startups turn to other distribution strategies, such as getting press coverage on the very blogs with whom you're competing for attention.

The challenge with getting press as a startup, small business, or online entrepreneur is that you're vying for the attention of media outlets that are constantly flooded with similar proposals.

A journalist friend of mine who works at a large media site in New York told me she gets anywhere from 25 to 30 emails per day requesting press coverage. Many of the requests aren't even relevant to her field. She's busy enough as it is, so she admits to deleting most of them without even reading them!

So how do you stand out in the Sea of Sameness?

Well, guest blogging, of course :)

Guest blogging is a great way to attract both large and targeted audiences to your business.

I've achieved a lot of success getting both traffic, email subscribers, and paying customers from guest blogging. I've been published on sites such as The Huffington Post, Entrepreneur, and The Next Web.

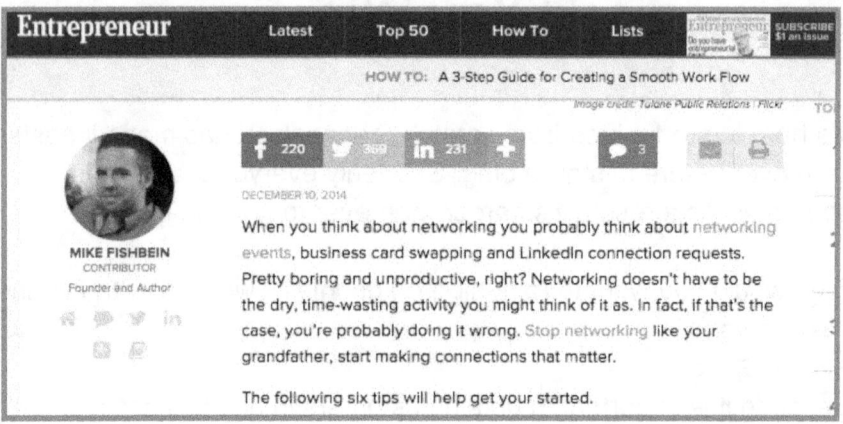

Guest blogging can bring immediate impact by putting you in front of a publication's existing audience. It can also help you over the long-term by enabling you to build links. Backlinks are a significant contributor to how pages rank on Google.

In addition, you get to craft your own story. You get to say what you want, as opposed to a journalist, who could misconstrue your message. As one journalist friend said:

"I was sent a request to write about an app that offered negative reinforcement to its user to encourage weight loss. The intention was to have me write something about its being funny or helpful, but when I checked out the app myself, I found that it was a really destructive way to lose weight."

Despite what you may have heard, not all press is good press. Journalists can write negative reviews about your product or site, and that won't help your sales at all. And hiring a PR agency can cost thousands of dollars, while guest blogging is free if you put in the effort.

But guest blogging hasn't been all the roses of traction and the butterflies of growth from the start for me. When I first pitched an editor of a popular site, I was I afraid I was going to get rejected and forever be branded a loser. Guest blogging was all so new to me, I couldn't bear the thought of something going wrong.

To my surprise, the editor was quite receptive. What I've come to realize is one of the biggest challenges people face when it comes to guest blogging is not their talent, ability to write, their company, or lack of audience, it's their own fear of rejection that holds them back.

One of my favorite quotes is, "*If you aren't getting rejected on a daily basis, your goals aren't ambitious enough,*" by Chris Dixon. If you're afraid of getting rejected, don't worry. That's completely normal. Our fears never go away no matter what we are doing. The best thing you can do is learn to overcome them on a daily basis.

So how do you approach guest blogging? There's a systematic formula that can get you from cold email to a published copy in front of a large audience of potential customers.

We'll dive into that over the course of that throughout this book. But before we do, I want to give you an understanding of what SEO is and how guest blogging can help, along with the importance of building your email list, how guest blogging can help you do it, and four other ways to grow your email list.

Chapter 2

SEO In Words So Simple A Baby Could Rank On Google

When done correctly, SEO can get you traffic, customers, and sales while you sleep. When done poorly, SEO won't benefit your website at all. If you're new to SEO, don't worry. In this section, I break it down for you in simple terms.

When I first started learning search engine optimization (SEO), I thought it was a foreign language created by rocket scientists-- some cruel mix of advanced mathematics and hieroglyphics or something.

SEO is indeed a very complex topic, but it's not as complex as people think, especially if they can think about it in the right way. We will provide essential SEO advice in relatively simple terms. In terms that really helped me to wrap my head around what SEO really is.

But does SEO even still work? Hasn't Google made it harder to "game" the system? What about all these "panda updates" - why bother trying?

Yes, Google has made it harder to make crappy content rank highly on its search engine. A lot of the quick hacks don't work anymore. But Google has not stopped being a starting point for people looking for information, and it has not stopped trying to provide searchers with the most relevant and high quality results.

Almost 12 billion searches are made on Google per month (and that's just 67.5% of the market). It's estimated that 64% of all web traffic comes from organic search. When one of the 1.17 billion people who search on Google each month search for something you offer, do they find you?

Let us dive deeper into how SEO works , what Google's job is, and important high impact hacks for getting the best ranking on Google.

What is Google's job?

What has helped me the most in understanding SEO is to first think about it in terms of what Google's job is. What is Google trying to accomplish?

Essentially, Google's job is to give searchers the most relevant and high quality search results. That's what searchers want, and that's probably why most of us use Google -- because we want to find information that's relevant to us when we search, and because Google does a great job of providing that.

That's Google's job -- they want to make sure they're giving back the best possible information, based on what we are searching for.

In order to improve its ability to return the most relevant and valuable information possible, Google needs to rank the tremendously massive amounts of content on the web by order of the quality and relevance to the searcher.

However, there is so much content on the web that Google could not possibly manually screen every site and rank it and of course that would be insane. So they use an algorithm to do it automatically. If you understand what that algorithm is, you can produce your content in a way that appeals to that algorithm and therefore make you show up higher in search results, and therefore ultimately get more traffic.

While the process of Google determining what is good and relevant content and what is bad content might change, its mission won't change. In fact, I think Google will continue to get better and better at surfacing the best content. Therefore, creating great content will always work. Content marketing and SEO are essentially becoming synonymous. In other words, if you want to rank high on search engines, you have to create awesome content.

How does Google determine rankings?

Instead of hiring a team of people to manually evaluate every page of every website available on the web to determine where it should rank on a nearly infinite number of potential searches, Google looks for indications that the content is relevant (given what was searched) and valuable. It uses many proxies or indicators for relevance and value. Some of the factors are matching keywords, popularity, whether it is linked to externally and a few more as well. So the tactics are really just to appeal to those factors.

Popularity indicators that Google uses. For example, Google+1s is actually one of the number one factors that will influence your search ranking on Google -- how many times it's been "+1'd" on Google Plus. So if you're not on Google+, and you're doing content marketing, you should be there. Another example is the number of Facebook likes, comments, and social shares. Link building is another massive one.

To improve a website's or page's ranking, a marketer can make some optimizations to tell Google that its site is the best result for the searcher. We'll get to some tactics you can use to boost your search ranking later.

Backlinks are like endorsements

Think about the real world. How do people find products and determine which are the best to buy? They often get recommendations from their friends.

When one site links to a page on another site, that's basically a recommendation. Many bloggers, myself included, link to external sources that either elaborate on key concepts, provide evidence for statements, or provide additional value to readers.

Google uses that as a proxy for quality. Links are like endorsements, and Google thrives on endorsements.

There are a number different ways to build links. There have been entire books written on it, but guest posting is one of my favorite ways to build links. Not only does it provide backlinks it has a number of other benefits which are discussed throughout this book.

One example is that guest blog posts on a big site will rank higher than the equivalent post on a different site. Big websites have more content and better SEO. So, when you guest post on their site, your post will rank higher for your targeted keywords than it would on a smaller site.

Link building

Guest posting is a great way to build links. Reach out to blogs in your space and offer to write a guest post. Link back to your domain or a page (i.e. blog post) contextually within the post, and/or in your bio section of the blog.

Press is another good medium, though more challenging, way to get linked to. If you are a startup or have accomplished something big, some blogs might be interested in writing about you. Most media companies have an email address or form for submitting news.

The last and most organic way to build links is to to simply create awesome content that is worthy of being linked.

What the heck is keyword research?

Search terms		Avg. monthly searches ?	Competition ?	Suggested... ?	Ad impr. s... ?	Add to plan
seo for beginners	⌐	1,000	Medium	$3.76	–	»
seo 101	⌐	880	Low	$30.29	–	»
seo for startups	⌐	110	High	$14.30	–	»
seo for entrepreneurs		– –		–	–	»

The next core SEO concept that is important to understand is "keyword research." As I mentioned, text relevancy is another factor used to determine what results to show to a searcher. For example, if you search for "sports scores," a blog post titled "sports scores" is probably going to be closer to what you want than one titled "zoo hours" (all other factors being equal).

Using Google Keyword Planner can help you increase the likelihood that you will be the answer to your customer's search queries. The tool will show you the exact words and terms that people are searching for, and how often, so that you can use those in your content.

For example, to determine what I should title this post, I came up with a few ideas for what someone who would be looking for a beginner's guide to SEO might be searching for. Google Keyword Planner then showed me how often each of those terms were searched, and provided some additional ideas about related searches that might be more relevant or create higher volume.

Why does this matter? It's much easier to get traffic when you know people are already searching for your content!

Keyword research, demystified

Research some keywords to determine what people are searching for as it pertains to your niche. Here are some things to look for when evaluating keywords:

a. Searches

If a large number of people are searching a given keyword, that's an indication there is demand for websites, pages, or content related to it. Google Keyword Planner measures and displays this as "Avg. monthly searches."

b. Intent

Does the keyword indicate buying intention? For example, "buy [product]", "hire a [profession]" or "[product] [size/specification]" is probably more likely to be from someone with the intent to buy. A search like "[product]" is probably from someone who is more in the research or casual browsing phase. "How to [activity]" shows more intent to learn how to do that activity than "[activity]." So if you're selling a book, or course, that could be a great term to target.

c. Competition

Little or no competition is probably a bad sign. It could mean there is money to be made in those keywords or another marketer is targeting them. Too much competition means it may be harder for you to rank for those terms.

Google Keyword Planner displays the relative competitiveness of the term in the "competition" column. In addition, the "suggested bid" column shows how much people are willing to pay for those clicks. It's likely the more someone is willing the pay the more money they're making back in return.

Do some qualitative research to see how strong your competition is. For example, if you search the keyword and multiple big name blogs come up, such as the New York Times, etc., it may be hard to compete with them. Conversely, if your search returns some small niche blogs, you may have a chance at outranking them.

The Quick Hacks

We provided some core principles, but ranking number one on Google would require an entire book so below are a few quick hacks to succeed on Google:

a. Use relevant, high volume, low competition keywords in your headlines, meta descriptions (you can learn more about these here), title, etc., to optimize your site.

b. Pick a domain that matches a keyword you want to rank for if possible, and doesn't completely sacrifice your image. A site's actual domain name has an effect on search rankings.

Having an exact match, .com domain name will provide a boost. For example, "turkeytrees.com" will rank higher than "bushchicken.io" when someone searches "turkey trees", all else being equal. .com, .net, and .org domains rank higher than other domain endings. Country relevant domain endings, such as .us, will rank higher for searches made in that given country.

Domains with numbers are penalized. Longer domains also rank lower than shorter domains.

c. Use WordPress. WordPress is a blogging platform that makes it really easy to improve SEO. It's easy to edit link structures, meta descriptions etc. Yoast, and other WordPress plugins make it easier to improve SEO.

d. Create awesome content that's valuable, not too short, and contains relevant keywords.

e. Build links by creating content that's worth linking to, and guest blogging.

Key Takeaways

Google was not the first search engine. In fact it was about the twelfth. It entered a highly competitive market, but managed to come out on top by having one crucial competitive advantage - providing searchers with the results it wanted. One of the biggest ways its process was different from other search engines was that it focused on ranking pages that had more links pointing to it.

There is so much content on the web, that Google cannot possibly manually screen every site and rank it. So it uses an algorithm to do it automatically. It's not always perfect, but given Google is the largest search engine and the number one site visited on the Web, people seem generally happy with the results they get when searching.

Before you start worrying about "meta data" and "h1 tags," understand the basics, and understand what search engines' ultimate goal is. While you won't learn everything you need to know in order to get your page ranking higher, the above information is pretty much the "80/20" of what you need to know.

There's a lot of stuff to know, but I gave you the most important and impactful information (20%) that will deliver of the best SEO results (80%) for your blog .

Search is not the only way to get traffic. You may not want to sacrifice on quality even if it means a slightly higher ranking, especially since as Google gets better at it's job, the hacks will have less effect. However, there are certainly many people searching on Google, so by "showing up," you can massively increase the amount of relevant traffic you get.

Chapter 3

How to Build Your Email List

The biggest mistake I've made in growing my business has been not focusing on building my email list. An email list is valuable for a number of reasons, the main one being communication with clients. Email marketing can sometimes even trump social media networking, and here's why. People get thousands of Facebook or Twitter posts in their feed a day, but only about a hundred emails in their inbox. It's harder to generate social media followers than it is an email list.

Email marketing is not dead. It is true that social media marketing has a lot to offer and is quite useful when appealing to the millennial generation, but the fact remains that more and more people are highly responsive to email marketing when done correctly.

Email marketing is personal. It takes marketing communications from a broadcast level to the inbox, where consumers feel more personal.

It's also direct. There are no news feeds, subscriptions, or hurdles to leap over. It's simple; you send content directly to their inbox.

While guest blogging is one of my favorite ways to get more email subscribers, there are a few other powerful ways. These strategies should be implemented in conjunction with or in addition to guest blogging.

Building your email list can not only help you get more traffic and sales, but it can help you get published on bigger and more reputable sites as a result.

How to get your first hundred email subscribers

A large and active email list is the lifeblood of any marketer in almost any kind of businesses.
More recently I've revamped my content strategy to focus on email opt ins and it's going swimmingly. Don't make the same mistakes I have. Here are the five strategies that have helped me the most in growing my email list:

1. Create awesome content

Just like if you build a product no one wants no one will use it, if you create content that no one wants, no one will read it. Creating awesome content is the basis for any content marketing strategy.

But what does "awesome" actually mean? Just like good software, good content solves a problem and delivers value to your audience. Make sure your content is relevant to your target audience, has attention grabbing titles, includes relevant keywords, and truly provides educational and/or entertainment value to your audience.

You can learn about all the strategies and tactics to discover what topics to produce content on here.

If you're creating content but your email list is not growing, you may have a content problem. If you're creating awesome content, but you're still not getting email subscribers, you may have a promotion problem. This leads to strategy number two....

2. Share content where your audience already is

If you have a new site and domain, publishing a new blog post might feel like talking to a wall. If you don't have a pre-existing audience who knows about your site, you'll need to go out and find an audience. Here are three ways to do that:

a. Share your content on your social channels, such as Google+, Twitter, Facebook, and LinkedIn. Posting in relevant LinkedIn groups, Google+ Communities, Twitter hashtags, and Facebook groups has also generated a lot of traffic and email subscribers.

b. Distribute your blog posts on content aggregation sites that are relevant to your industry. Some sites I share on are Inbound.org, GrowthHackers, Hacker News, Reddit, USV.com, and Quibb.

c. Consider blogging on platforms like LinkedIn, Medium, or Quora if you have followers there. If you don't have followers there, guest blogging might be your best option. More on that later.

3. Email opt in giveaways

What email lists do you subscribe to? Why do you subscribe? I'm going to guess it's because they send awesome emails.

By offering something valuable to people, instead of merely saying "give me your email address," you can increase your conversion rates. Make sure what you're offering is valuable to your audience.

I just started using ConvertKit to make the process of gathering email subscribers and giving away content easier. You can see an example of how I do this at the bottom of this post.

4. Tools of the trade

Here are the three tools that have been most beneficial to me in growing my email list:

a. SumoMe – social share buttons to get more traffic, pop up windows to collect emails, and more.

b. Mailchimp – I use the Mailchimp WordPress plugin to display an email optin box on every page of my site.

c. ConvertKit – I recently started using ConvertKit to build squeeze pages and create opt in forms to embed on my blog posts with giveaways.

5. Guest blogging

As software makes it cheaper and easier to create content, and content marketing grows in popularity, it's becoming harder to build massive audiences. Fortunately you can reap the fruits of other sites' labors by simply guest blogging on their site.

By guest blogging on a site whose audience is similar to yours, you can quickly reach a large number of potential subscribers. In addition, when a site with a high pagerank links to your site ("backlink"), you page rank increases. This means you will rank higher on Google search results and get more organic traffic.

Guest blogging is an amazing way to get traffic and email subscribers. That's why I've written this entire book dedicated to describing how I've published on top sites like *Entrepreneur, The Huffington Post, Business Insider,* and *The Next Web.*

Chapter 4

Public Relations and Other Marketing Strategies

After reading about email marketing and SEO, you might be thinking "Can't I accomplish all that through public relations? Why don't I just get Buzzfeed to write about me and then wait for the cash to roll in?"

I have had some success with public relations. And I do believe it can work for some businesses. But not all, and probably not in isolation.

Below you will find my best advice for getting press coverage on top sites, along with some advice from some experts in my network along with comparison of public relations and guest blogging as a marketing channel for startups and small businesses.

The truth about getting press

After building something people want, acquiring customers is often one of the biggest challenges a startup faces.

Press seems like a great option to many entrepreneurs. It seems so easy...you just have to get a journalist to write about you. You don't even have to write the article, and then boom--traction!

But is getting press really the holy grail of startup marketing? There are many benefits of PR discussed below.

a.) Search Engine Optimization (SEO)

An article on a big high ranking domain like Entrepreneur.com will rank much higher on Google than the equivalent article on your newly launched Tumblr blog. In addition, getting linked to (backlinks) has one of the biggest impact on a domain's search result ranking. So you're more likely to be found by someone searching on Google after getting press.

b.) Exposure

If the site you get covered by has a lot of active readers, you can get a ton of exposure. It can take a lot of time and money to build up an audience on your own blog, but when you get covered by a big site you get access to the fruits of their labor. Their audience might click through to your site from the article, providing you with some traffic.

c.) Credibility

When a reputable site talks about your company in a positive light, it can boost your credibility in the eyes of your customers. If your audience trusts a given source, and that source vouches for you, your audience might therefore gain trust for you.

This all sounds great, right? But are there any downsides to public relations for startups? Could there be any more efficient or effective ways to get customers? Is getting covered on Techcrunch the solution to your startup's traction problem? Here are some important considerations:

1. Big media journalists are hard to reach

Journalists at big media companies like Techcrunch or The New York Times are getting slammed by cold emails from startups just like you. We know you're a special snowflake, but the journalists might not.

It can take a lot of time to get press. Running a press campaign is similar to running a sales campaign. It often takes a lot of following up, building a relationship over time, and/or a warm referral from a person they trust in order to get in the door.

If you're a bootstrapped early stage startup, it's your time. Your time could be spent on the million other things you could be doing as a founder. If you're in the later stages, it will be employees' time, which costs money.. Or you might hire a public relations firm...

2. Hiring a public relations firm is expensive

It's not that complicated to reach out to journalists and get press, but if you feel your time could be better spent on other things, or if you really have no idea to do it, you might want to outsource it to a public relations (PR) firm.

A PR firm might have some good relationships or be better at crafting your pitch. However most of them charge a flat fee, so you pay regardless of whether or not you get coverage.

3. Big media outlets don't always have your audience

Many entrepreneurs read Techcrunch. Techcrunch does indeed have a large audience. But do your customers read Techcrunch?

Getting covered in Techcrunch might attract potential hires or investors, but if your customers aren't techies, it probably won't move the needle much in terms of traffic. Though backlinks are still good.

To maximize your efforts, you can start by creating a customer persona. Determine what your audience reads by conducting customer development interviews, using audience intelligence tools, or searching relevant terms on Google.

4. Sometimes smaller blogs can be more accessible

In the age of the Internet, podcasts are the new radio stations, YouTube is the new TV, Twitter is the new newspaper, and blogs are (not so) miniature media companies.

As discussed above, some of the big companies are overwhelmed with inquiries about getting coverage. However, sometimes the smaller or newer sites are more hungry for content. In addition, while they might not have as large of an audience, the audience might be highly relevant.

5. Lesser known media outlets often have sizable, and/or highly relevant audiences

As the Internet makes it cheaper and easier to start a media company, competition has heated up. Following classic business strategies, media companies and blogs are increasingly focusing on specific niches. For example, I focus on startup marketing rather than the entire field of marketing, or the entire field of startups.

The more focused the topic is, the more focused the audience. While smaller, more focused sites might have a smaller total audience size, a higher percentage of them might be relevant to you, and they might even have a higher total number of relevant people.

6. Better return on investmentment (ROI) because of ease

Is big media right for you?

Big media sites tend to cover big innovative ideas, companies backed by reputable investors, run by well-known and accomplished teams, operating in a new or exciting market, or reaching a major traction milestone. If you don't meet this criteria, it might take a lot of time and/or money (in terms of hiring a PR agency) to get published.

However, because smaller sites might have a more relevant audience, and might be accessible, targeting smaller sites might have a higher ROI than big media sites.

7. Press is not the only marketing channel

Tired of having your emails ignored by journalists? Don't have the budget for a fancy PR agency?

There are many ways to get website traffic and acquire customers. You could start your own blog, guest blog on someone else's blog, use social media, do direct sales, product content on other platforms, etc.

8. Guest blogging might be better than press

Does blogging on your own site feel like a fart in the wind?

If you really want the link juice and exposure, but you can't get journalists interested in writing about you, guest blogging might be a great alternative. You can get much of the benefit that press provides, possibly more, and possibly at a lower cost.

Guest blogging is when a site publishes a blog post you wrote and cites you. Most blogs will allow you to link to your website and/or relevant blog posts a couple times within the post and in your bio.

Guest blogging has the added benefits of enabling you to control your message (you write it, not them), and it is usually easier to get the attention of a blog by offering them content rather than asking them to write about you.

Key Takeaways and Next Steps

Once you know who your customers are, think about what they read. Depending on what they read, public relations might help you get there, or guest blogging might be better. You can also of course do both.

Press can help you with customer acquisition, but it also comes at a cost. Guest blogging can provide a better return on investment. Guest blogging has many benefits, which you can learn about by signing up below.

What do the experts say?

I've been on both sides of this double edged sword – trying to get press, and trying to get guest blog posts published.

Press sounds so promising. And prestigious. But it can also be expensive and time consuming. Guest blogging on the other hand requires creating the content and some "know how."

I certainly have my preferences, but my experiences only provide a limited amount of data. So I wanted to bring in some experts to share their experiences and help you decide whether PR or guest blogging is best for you.

The reality is, it really depends on what business you are in, among other factors. Here's what the experts say about those factors:

One or the other?

Matthew Capala, Founder of Alphametic, Blogger at SearchDecoder, NYU Professor, and Author of SEO Like I'm 5, illustrates how guest blogging can actually lead to press:

"Guest blogging and public relations have become two sides of the same coin. Through guest blogging you build your brand and following, which leads to media mentions, and eventually to becoming a resource for journalists. Yet, many businesses take a reversed approach, they hire PR firms to pitch their startup to media before developing their message and building a following around it.

For example, I published one of the chapters of my book, SEO Like I'm 5, on the The Next Web, The Good, The Bad, and The Ugly of SEO, which was then covered by the Chicago Tribune and translated into French. Not only did I scored high-profile media mentions through guest blogging, but also it has helped me generated a lot of business."

Creating great content is an effective way to market your business and can lead to many revenue-generating opportunities. It's also important to acknowledge that guest blogging and public relations don't need to be a "one or the other" proposition.

The Importance of relationships

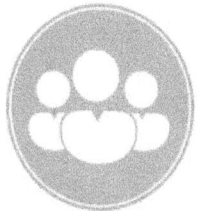

Ivana Taylor, a publication owner who receives pitches constantly, illustrates how PR can provide value:

"This is a pet subject for me since I get pitches from PR people ALL THE TIME for guest posts and I have to tell you that it's really annoying. See this article for details.

When I think about paying for PR — what I'm buying isn't a set of TASKS – what I'm buying is the PR professionals RELATIONSHIPS with media (which could include bloggers). Unfortunately, I don't think small business owners consider this when hiring PR folks because I am constantly getting pitched for what I call one-pitch-stands.

As a small business influencer and blogger – I IGNORE those because I'm looking for a relationship with experts and the PR person — so that the content is directed to my audience and the audience can trust the expert and their advice.

Guest blogging is great when your product or service is a TIGHT match for the blogger. Honestly, the only way to know that is to have read and interacted with the blog. This will not only increase your chances of being published, it will increase the promotional attention that the blogger will give your content."

Ivana's points about focusing on building long-term relationships, providing value through great content, and finding the right sites to get published on are extremely important, applying both to public relations and guest blogging.

Public Relations is expensive

If you don't have the time, relationships, or know-how to do public relations yourself, you'll have to hire a PR firm. For a startup, this can be a considerable blow to remaining runway.
Amy Vernon, Co-founder & CMO of Predictable.ly talks about what to look for in a PR firm and acknowledges the risk of a PR firm making too many promises:

"A lot of PR folks claim relationships they don't have. When I was a journalist, I dealt with some terrific folks in public relations and some really horrible ones who sent out copies of the same press release to the entire newsroom, not caring if it made sense or not. You need to do your research before hiring and not just take the firm's word that they get results. Too many do not."

Many PR firms don't work on a contingent basis. So you pay regardless if you get published. Conversely, if you pay someone to make content for you to guest blog, you will almost definitely get content back.

Reputation and prestige

Amy Vernon illustrates the reputation value that public relations can provide.

"In Public Relations, the value is someone who understands how to properly craft messages and who has the right relationships to get you visibility. Despite the decline of "traditional" media, getting a mention in print in Vogue or USA Today or Time carries a certain caché, because there's still a finite amount of space in the dead-tree editions. And those mentions are online as well, usually."

I think the reputation value of being covered by a major publication can be especially valuable to b2b startups. Someone at a big company needs to be able to trust that you won't break too many things.

Factors to consider

Kathy Murray, of McMorran Strategists, provides a framework for how to decide on the right strategy based on your business:

"1. Begin with what is the product? Who are the potential customers? B2B, B2C or some combination? Any potential partners that the startup wants to attract?
2. What do these potential customers read or follow – Facebook, LI, Twitter, Blogs, Instagram, and dare we say it – print newspapers/magazines – etc.? Are they geographically dispersed?
3. What is your content? About the product? The industry?
4. What is your following on social media?
5. Then, one decides how to spend their limited resources of TIME and $'s."

This illustrates the point that the choice between guest blogging is not the same for every company. In particular, I think it's important to consider who your target customers are.

Does your target audience read where you would be getting press? Your audience might not read sites that do press releases and cover stories about startup businesses. For example, if your customers are moms in the midwest, they might not be reading Techcrunch.

Your target market might read publications that don't do press releases or coverage stories. They might read sites focused on educational content instead. If this is the case, a press release about a product launch or funding milestone might not provide as much value or build rapport as effectively as a guest post that provides educational or entertainment value.

What's your story?

Not every business is worthy of being covered by a journalist. Journalists like to cover the most exciting and innovative companies and stories.

You need to have news in order to get coverage - exciting news in particular.

A self-published book, or a web development agency might not be very exciting to a journalist.

However, valuable educational content is almost always of interest to many publications.

Therefore, it may be easier for a business without a major milestone to get published on a site by guest blogging rather than by pitching a PR story.

You can publish valuable content at any time. Guest blogging provides a consistent pulse of content being published over time and across multiple outlets.

Next steps

I have done public relations campaigns that have landed features on sites like VentureBeat and more. However, I have been published on a higher quantity and quality of sites and gained more results from guest blogging. But I wanted to make sure I wasn't alone in this experience, and make sure you received both sides of the story.

Chapter 5

How to Figure Out Where to Guest Blog

If you've read this far, you know that guest blogging can produce great returns, in terms of traffic, backlinks, and email subscribers. But what sites should you be guest blogging on?

In this chapter and the following you'll discover the step-by-step process I've taken to get published on sites like Entrepreneur, The Next Web and The Huffington Post.

Before you can hit a target you have to know where to aim. Before getting published you need to know where you should be pitching in the first place.

To get the best results, you want to guest blog on sites that your audience reads, that accept guest posts, and generate a lot of traffic. But how do you figure out what sites meet those criteria?

This post covers a five-step strategy for determining the best sites to guest blog:

1. Who are your customers?

You can't know where to guest blog unless you know who you're trying to reach. For an early stage startup, it may take some testing to determine who exactly

Here are a couple questions I like to ask to determine what the target customer segment(s) might be:
Who is most severely affected by the problem your content is solving?

Who would absolutely love to read your article? Think very specifically.

For example, people who might find this post about guest blogging include beginner to immediate bloggers concerned with getting more traffic and backlinks and boosting SEO. Another would be early stage software entrepreneurs who are using content marketing to acquire customers.

If Help a Reporter Out was solving the problem of link building, they might guest blog on an SEO blog. An SEO blog's audience is likely to be interested in link building.

2. What do your customers read?

The next step after figuring out who your customers are is to go where they go. As it pertains to guest blogging, you want to get published on the sites that they are already reading. It will be a lot easier to attract customers if you get in where they already are (instead of trying to pull them to you).

You want to figure out what sites your customers read, and are relevant to the product, service, and/or content you provide. Here are a few ways to figure out what your customers are reading:

a. Customer development interviews

Customer development can be used beyond just validating business ideas. Yay! Asking your customers what they read is a great way to figure out where to guest blog.

Here are some customer development questions I have asked to figure out what people read: What are your favorite blogs? What are your favorite news sites? What sites do you read for news and educational content related to your industry?

Sometimes it's as simple as just asking your customers.

b. Search on Google

Search for the words your customers are likely to be searching for. For example, if your customers are content marketers, you could search "content marketing", or "content marketing blog" to make sure you are finding sites that are blogs. You could also search for the specific topic(s) of your article, such as guest blogging, email marketing, public relations, etc..

Before you search, make sure you're searching the right terms -- the terms that are being searched by your audience. You might be surprised by what you find. I thought that "startup ideas" would be a common search term, but it turned out that "business ideas" was about ten times more common.

Start with google keyword planner to determine what those common search keywords and phrases even are. Enter in some ideas and the tool will show you how much search volume it gets and make suggestions for other relevant and popular search terms.

c. Audience Intelligence tools

If you have an email list and/or social following you can learn more about your audience and what they read. There are some very powerful, and expensive audience intelligence tools that can tell you a lot about who your customers are. I'm cheap, so I don't have a lot of experience with those, but I have received much value from a couple of other free tools.

One simple, free and easy to use audience intelligence tool is analytics.twitter.com. Go to the "followers" tab. There you can see what your audience's interests are and who they are commonly following. This can give you an idea of what kinds of sites specifically you might use to find similar people.

Interests

Most unique interests ⑦

68% Entrepreneurship

61% Startups

54% Business and finance

43% Marketing

42% Leadership

Your followers also follow

31% TechCrunch · Profile

31% mashable · Profile

31% hootsuite · Profile

30% StartupPro · Profile

28% LollyDaskal · Profile

27% ManagersDiary · Profile

27% FastCompany · Profile

26% JonahLupton · Profile

25% 2morrowknight · Profile

As you can see, there are a few blogs on my list. Maybe the individuals on the list have blogs of their own. Those could be great sites for me to guest blog on.

Another tool is Followerwonk, where you can search Twitter bios by your target keywords, rank people by their influence, and see if they have blogs that accept guest posts.

Using this strategy, make sure your followers are within your target customer segment (not always true because there is so much spam on Twitter hah.), and still do some qualitative due diligence on the sites you find.

3. What sites accept guest posts?

It's important to find not just any sites, but sites that actually accept guest posts. Not all sites accept guest or contributor posts. Here are two ways you can determine if a site accepts guest posts:

a. Look for a "contact" page or "contribute" page. Look at the top headings or at the bottom footer of the websites.

b. Search the site name + write for us. For example, for http://www.socialmediaexplorer.com/. I searched "Social Media Explorer write for us" and found this http://www.socialmediaexplorer.com/how-to-pitch-sme/. You can also try searching "site name + contribute." For example, "Social Media Explorer contribute"

Write for Us: Contributor Guidelines

Thanks for your interest in writing for The Write Life!

Before you submit, please run through this checklist. Have you...

Take note of their policies on how to pitch, what to pitch, etc.. We'll come back to that later.

4. What sites have the best reach?

You might find a site that's completely relevant to your topic and your audience, and accepts guest posts, but if they are too small, they might not provide a good return on investment. To qualify potential places to guest post, there are a few metrics you can look at:

a. Pagerank. The higher the better.They provide better backlinks for you. Plus, as I discussed in chapter 2, the post itself will rank higher on Google than the equivalent post on a lower page ranking site. Also, a higher page ranking site is likely to have more traffic, landing you more reads and potential click throughs to your website. Two sites you can use to check a site's authority are Moz's open site explorer and CheckPageRank.net

b. Email subscribers. Not all sites disclose this publicly, some don't even disclose this privately. But the larger a site's email list, the more views your post is likely to get.

c. Social following. How many Twitter followers, Facebook likes, etc. do they have? Some sites get a significant amount of their traffic from their social channels, so if they have a large social following, guest posting there can get more traffic to the guest post because they will almost definitely share it on their social channels.

d. Reputation. One benefit of being published on big sites is that it can improve your reputation. What are your customers' perception of the site? If you are a B2B software company, publishing on Buzzfeed might not be viewed as favorably by your customers as being published on a site like *The Wall Street Journal*.

5. Pitch, Test, Track, Repeat

To briefly summarize, you want a site that is read by your target audience, has a lot of traffic and high page rank, and will accept your guest post. You can never know for sure which sites will accept or produce the best results. Like so many other aspects of business, it requires testing.

That's why the next and final step is simply to pitch and see what sites accept and what produce the best outcomes for you. After you've found some sites that meet the above criteria, see which ones will accept your content, and which produce the best results.

I certainly haven't been published by 100% of the sites I've pitched to. I probably haven't even been published by half of the sites I've pitched to. Some of my guest posts have landed me a lot of traffic, email subscribers, and juicy backlinks, and some haven't. But by testing and interpreting I can now double down on what's working.

To increase your chances of being accepted by top sites, create awesome content and follow the instructions the site gives on how they preferred to be pitched. If the big sites aren't accepting your guest posts, you can start with smaller, but still relevant sites and climb your way up.

Chapter 6

How to Get Published on Top Sites

If you've read this far, you have a good understanding of the benefits of guest blogging, and content marketing and SEO in general, and how to figure out where to guest blog. If you've skipped around, go back and get caught up!

So, now you're probably wondering how your guest posts gets published on that huge site that all your customers read. Well, this is the chapter for you.

1. Create a prospect list

For guest blogging to be effective, you need to go where your target market is, and in order to get your content published, you need to go to sites that publish your kind of content. Based on your research above, create a list of potential places to guest post.

Your prospect list can look much like a CRM, a comprehensive list of places you want to write for, with the ability to track your communication with the site (getting published can sometimes require many follow-ups).

2. Create awesome content

As you might expect any blog worth publishing on is going to want to publish high quality content. In a world where everyone is a blogger, it's more important than ever to create content that truly provides value to your audience.

To make sure I'm producing content that my audience finds valuable, I apply Lean startup principles and customer development tactics to create content. I use customer development tactics to learn about what people's problems are, how I can provide value to them, and what tests can be implemented to make sure my content meets their needs.

I apply Lean by running experiments and producing content iteratively to spend too much time and money on something my customers won't find valuable.

Some of the specific things to determine content topics that are more likely to deliver results are to field questions from my readers, look at what content your competition is producing that is performing well, doing keyword research to see what people are searching for, looking at what content on platforms like Amazon are performing well, and writing blog posts about given topics before writing an entire book and gaining feedback as you go.

I won't go too deep into this since I wrote an entire Ebook on it already. You can read that for free here.

Two Forms of Value

According to the definition above, content must be valuable to the target audience. What does it mean to be valuable? Value, as it pertains to content marketing, comes in two primary forms:

a. Entertainment value

The audience finds the content funny, interesting, or otherwise entertaining. The best example of content marketing that has entertainment value is Dollar Shave Club's video that now has over thirteen million views. People watched it, even multiple times, and shared it, because they enjoyed watching it. The fact that it's an advertisement is an afterthought. In addition, it improves Dollar Shave Club's brand by making them look "cool."

b. Educational value

The audience finds the content helpful. It answers their questions or gives them information that they can use to solve their problems or in some way improve themselves. The best example of content marketing that I can think of that has educational value is *Moz's Beginner's Guide to SEO*. It is like the Bible for beginning SEO. It is the go-to source for anyone that wants to learn SEO. The fact that Moz did it to attract their target audience - marketers - is not even recognized at first glance. In addition, it improves Moz's brand by displaying their expertise, and building a perception of being helpful.

So which kind of value should you provide? Both! Provide "edu-tainment". Your awesome content should be both valuable and entertaining.

3. Pitch, Fail, Repeat Until Success

Some people recommend pitching an idea or a title before sending the entire post, but from my experience, I've had better reception when I send over a draft of the entire post. I recommend experimenting with this, and of course following the guidelines of each site.

Here's an example of an email I've sent to an editor:

Subject: Guest post on [site name] - writing habit for content creation

"Hi [name]

Would CMI be interested in a guest blog post on content writing?

I'm Mike, I'm the self-published author of over half a dozen books including How to Write a Book in 10 Days:123 Quick Tips for Fast Non-Fiction Self-Publishing and have had my writing featured on Huffington Post, Entrepreneur, Business Insider, and Convince and Convert

I would love to guest post about making writing a habit, overcoming writer's block, writing faster, etc.. Below is a link to a draft of a post titled "6 Steps to Developing a Daily Writing Habit."

[link to Google Doc]

Do you think this would make for a good guest post on [site name]?

Thanks,
Mike"

They key elements are as follows: a) Make a clear ask at the beginning and end of the email, b) Introduce yourself and state some accomplishments to build authority, social proof, and rapport, c) Mention the article, what it's about and why you think it's valuable, and d) Link to the complete post in Google Drive.

If and when you get published, be sure to share it on your social channels and reply to any comments, as this may make the site more inclined to have you publish there again. Once you've been published on a few smaller blogs it can be easier to reach out to bigger names. The more bylines you have the more leverage you have to be chosen by a bigger site.

4. Network

Sometimes it's not just how good your writing is, but who you know. Having a referral from someone an editor trusts can be a great way to motivate them to publish you.

I became a regular contributor to *The Huffington Post* as a result of a long chain of networking events, connections, and follow ups. In another chapter I will tell you about how exactly I got into *The Next Web* through networking and referrals. Here's the story about how I became a contributor at *Huffington Post*:

It started with a workshop. I wasn't even sure that it would be a good workshop. The teacher seemed underqualified and there were a million other things I could be doing with my time.

But, I went anyway because I knew I needed to make a lot of things happen. I needed to increase my chances of getting lucky -- I needed to manufacture serendipity.

It turned out to be a great workshop. I met the teacher. I'm still friends with one of the other students.

I followed up with the teacher. He happened to be the best networker I had met. And inspired me to really make networking a priority and informed some of my strategies. We became friends. We are still good friends.

After a few months of hanging out and staying in touch, he invited me to an event. He didn't really explain what the event was, so I wasn't sure if it would be good, but I went anyways because I trusted his judgement and I wanted to continue to make a lot of things happen.

It turned out to be an amazing event. It was a private book launch party for Reid Hoffman, co-founder of LinkedIn, and his new book The Startup of You. It was hosted by Mayor Bloomberg. I met the President of MTV and some startup founders.

I was talking to an entrepreneurs I had met that night, just an hour or two earlier. "Hey there's Arianna Huffington, let's go talk to her," he said.

My initial reaction was anxiety. But I turned off my brain, reminded myself of how important it was to get out there, and I went and talked to her. I think I was on autopilot.

I was incredibly nervous. I didn't even feel worthy.

I don't even remember what we talked about, but eventually she offered to have me contribute to her site, The Huffington Post. I got her email address.

The next day I followed up, but I was still nervous.

I emailed her asking if I could contribute, as she had suggested. She said yes and introduced me to an editor via email.

This has since led me to more opportunities for both business and guest blogging. The backlinks and traffic I have received from Huffington Post definitely made the networking worth-while.

5. Climb The Ladder

It sounds so rad to get published on the biggest sites in your industry. And don't get me wrong, it can deliver some incredible results, but smaller, highly relevant sites, can produce great results. In addition, getting published on smaller sites can help you build your reputation, social proof and track record.

Sometimes it helps when pitching to editors to be able to say you've been published on at least one other at least moderately reputable site in the past.

If the post on a smaller site performs really well (for example, if it gets a lot of shares and the site displays that number), an editor may be more enticed to publish you. Remember, these sites make money by getting lots of traffic to the site. The editor's job is to produce and source content that will drive traffic to the site. If your content has produced much traffic in the past, there is less guess work in the editor's mind.

6. Follow instructions

One sure fire way to start off on the wrong foot with an editor is to not follow their instructions for pitching. Every site has different preferences for being pitched. Make sure you read their page and adapt accordingly. There are a couple ways to find this page:

a. Look for a "contact" page or "contribute" page. This is usually either located on top headings or at the bottom footer of the websites.

b. Search the site name + write for us. For example, for Social Media Explorer. I searched "Social Media Explorer write for us" and found this http://www.socialmediaexplorer.com/how-to-pitch-sme/. You can also try searching "site name + contribute." For example, "Social Media Explorer contribute."

Most sites will ask you to send a description of the article or the full article, along with your biography. Some sites have a contact form; others will give you an email address. Some sites will tell you what kind of content they are looking for along with requirements about length or links.

7. Be persistent

I thought business was all about "vision" and "creativity." It turns out so much of it is just about sending many follow-up emails. I can't tell you how much money I've made from simply sending follow-up emails.

They say execution is everything. Following up is execution.

It's annoying. But it works. If it didn't work, I wouldn't do it. And I wouldn't encourage you to do it. But it does. So I do.

For example, it took me months of following up with *Entrepreneur* before I got published. They didn't allow me to become a regular contributor until I published a couple posts that did well. Now that I've proved myself, I'm able to get published there much more easily.

If they say no, don't keep following up.

Don't get discouraged if you get a response that looks like this:

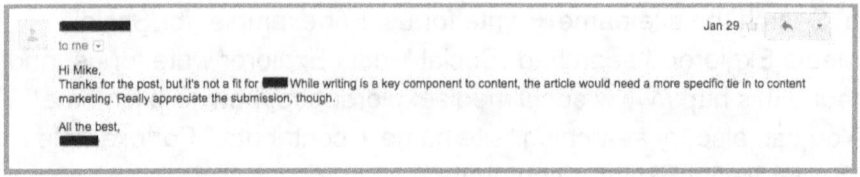

Instead, be patient, because eventually you'll get a response that looks like this:

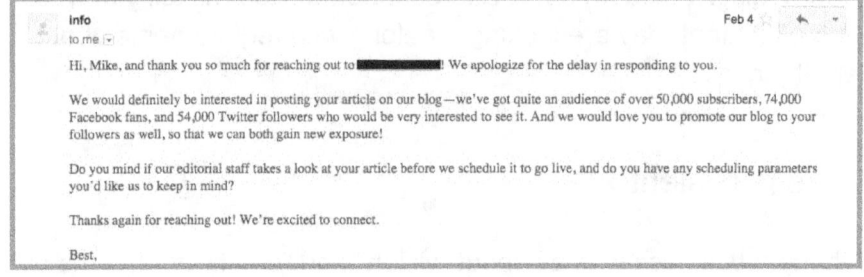

Chapter 7

My 100+ Lead Guest Blogging Case Study

So, I've given you the nuts and bolts on guest blogging, and it's a lot to digest, I know. But, I really want you to understand this stuff so you can start using it to grow your business. So, here's a case study that demonstrates real life examples based on the principles in this book. It'll show you how I used one guest blog post to generate over 100 qualified leads within a couple days.

Backstory: I was working for a business to business software as a service company doing inbound marketing and lead generation. We had very few email subscribers and we weren't getting as much traffic as we wanted.

This is a classic example of how guest blogging very quickly helped boost our search ranking (we were a pagerank 0 at the time), land e-mail subscribers, and get lots of traffic. And it's still generating new email opt-ins!

Here were our goals going into this guest blogging campaign:

1. Get in front of massive amounts of our target market

It can take years and mounds of blog posts before building a substantial audience on your own blog. Fortunately there are sites out there who have already spent those years and millions of dollars to build an audience of people you want to reach. And you can reap the benefits of their hard work by partnering with them.

2. Build links that will boost search ranking

SEO is a complicated topic that I covered in more detail in the previous chapter, but know this: getting linked to by another site is one of the most impactful inputs of Google's search algorithm.

Here's how it helped us:

Here are the exact steps I took to get published on *The Next Web* and generate massive amounts of traffic and email subscribers.

The Next Web is a large and highly relevant site for us. They write about topics of interest to our target audience, and are therefore commonly read by our target audience.

As you can see below, they have a huge following, high page rank, and steady traffic. To be specific, they have over one million Twitter followers, a pagerank of 7, and get 6.5 million unique visitors per month (reported as of May 2015).

Knowing that a backlink from them would boost our SEO, and that getting shared on their site and social channels would give us a lot of relevant exposure and traffic, it was a perfect site for a guest post..

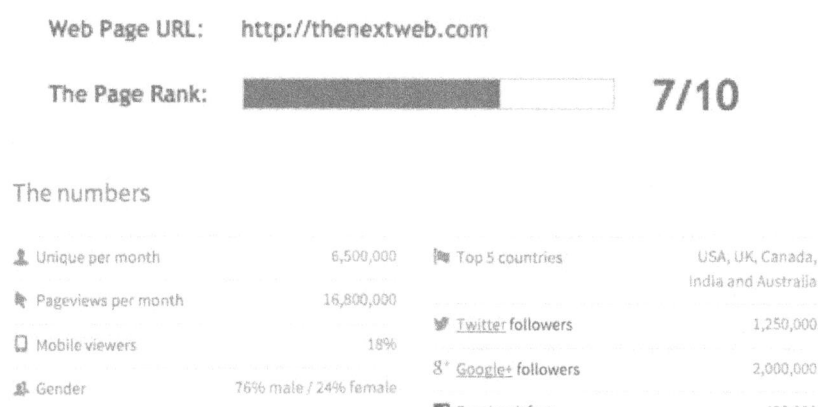

Step one: Produce epic content

The first thing we did, as I have preached throughout this book, is produce content that solves a problem and delivers value to our target audience. In the case it was an ebook about trends in Product Management that we had already written.

Step two: Break it into blog posts

Next we broke up the ebook into a few blog posts that provided value discretely.

Here's a lesson I learned the hard way: don't go straight to producing "epic" content without validation. Make sure the ebook provides value, or else you won't convert the traffic you get from the guest posts, and the guest posts themselves probably won't get as much traffic, and might not even get accepted by any sites. Conversely, if your book rocks, your guest posts will rock, and therefore you should get more traffic and a higher conversion rate to email subscribers.

Step three: Pitch to an editor

Once we had a blog post ready, we pitched it to an editor at *The Next Web*. I almost always send cold emails, but in this case, I was able to get introduced to someone at the company.

To get the warm introduction, I started by logging on to LinkedIn and navigating to *The Next Web* company page. Next, I browsed the list of all the employees at the company to see which ones I had shared connections.

I had a shared connection to the Director of Business Development, so I asked our shared connection if he knew him well and would feel comfortable making an introduction. The shared connection did indeed make the introduction.

Once the connection was made via email, I sent the Director of Business Development a link to the draft of the post in Google Drive, and asked him if he could connect me to an editor. He did connect me to an editor.

The editor must have liked the draft, because they decided to publish it.

Step four: Get published, and make it rain

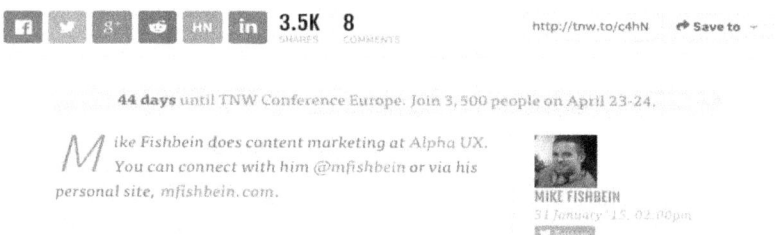

Within the post, we contextually linked to the squeeze page for the entire ebook. The squeeze page looked similar to this below.

Within the first few weeks it generated hundreds of leads.

But we didn't stop there.

We wrote the "Meta" post and guest blogged that.

We wrote about the marketing strategy and the results it delivered, and guest blogged that article. This one didn't produce as strong of results, which usually means there's something to be learned. But first, some background...

Survey Money is almost a competitor, so they are likely to have an audience that's relevant to us. In addition they are a pagerank 9. That is very high. Not even some of the biggest media sites are that high. To put it in more perspective: My blog is a 3 pushing on 4 and we were a 0 at the time.

So clearly they're doing a great job building the blog, and it would be great to get some of that link juice.

The results of this campaign ended up being sub-par because it was not relevant to our audience. It was definitely a valuable post, but it wasn't targeted to people who wouldn't be interested in the ebook. Therefore, the people that read the post were not signing up very frequently.

As you can see from the above screenshot, the title and the content were not directly relevant to our target market, i.e. product managers.

While it did not produce much traffic or email subscribers in the short-term, the long term benefit, in terms of SEO, ended up being great because SurveyMonkey had and has such a high page rank.

Lessons learned: don't just create content that is valuable, create content that is relevant.

Strategy recap

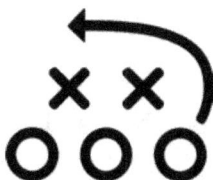

The post on *The Next Web* continues to generate leads and traffic and is of course indexed by Google, so it will rank higher in search results than an equivalent post on our site. In addition, the backlinks we earned will continue to pay dividends.

Here are the key takeaways from this experience:

1. Go where your audience goes
2. Attract and engage them with relevant and valuable content
3. Convert them into customers or leads by linking to a squeeze page
4. Epic content —> micro content guest blogged (link back to epic content)

The short-term benefit of guest blogging is that you get in front of large quantities of your target audience. The long-term benefit is SEO (your site will rank higher because of the backlinks). The content on *The Next Web* will continue to be viewed, and our reputation and track record has improved, which can increase our chances of getting published on other sites.

There is almost nothing better than free, automated lead generation!

Key Takeaways

If you can't beat 'em join 'em. Instead of trying to compete with blogs that already have your target audience, guest blogging is a great way to get your business out there by tapping into a pre-existing audience. A lot of startups try to get press, but guest blogging might be the better solution to getting customers.

Getting traffic is hard. Really hard. If you build it they will not necessarily come.

There are many ways to get traffic and acquire customers. Some of the more popular strategies include sales, partnerships, social media marketing, content marketing, public relations, blogging, and guest blogging.

Each of these strategies are challenging for different reasons. But I think guest blogging has a great balance between difficulty and results it can deliver.

Guest blogging is a great way to execute on a larger content marketing strategy. The principles of content marketing apply to and lend themselves to guest blogging. When guest blogging, consider the below core concepts.

Guest blogging is great for SEO because you build links and a blog post on a high page rank site will rank higher on Google than an equivalent post on a lower ranking site. It's great for gaining relevant traffic because you get in front of large numbers of your target audience and can direct them back to your website.

Every industry and every business is different. Some people are better at producing text content than video content and therefore may get better results from blogging. There is no way to know for sure what strategy is best for your business.

If you are unsure, spend some time seeing what is working for your competitors, and making an educated hypothesis about what will work best for you. Like I said, you can never know for sure, so when in doubt, test it.

It is likely that you will have to try a couple different marketing channels to see what will work for you. Content marketing, and guest blogging in particular, has worked for me. Here is some of my biggest advice about content marketing:

Three big pieces of content marketing advice

1. Create content that's valuable to your audience! If you do that, people will find you, share your content, engage with you, return to your site, etc. In an ever-increasing competitive world, it's more important than ever to produce content that is unique and truly solves a problem.

2. Go where your audience goes. Produce content on the platforms discussed in this book if your audience spends time there.

3. Capture your audience. Don't just produce content for the sake of producing content. Produce it to get results. Engage with the people who find your content and turn them into customers. Building an email list is a great way to do this.

Next steps -- find time, make sure the content rocks, and tap into even more networks. The free resources below will help you with just that.

Additional Resources

There are two additional ingredients you need to truly achieve great success with guest blogging and content marketing. Those two ingredients are awesome content, and the time to write it.

I know my readers like concise content that solves a specific problem and doesn't waste their time with anything they might not want. So I didn't include those topics in this book. I feel this book does a great job of solving one specific problem: learning how to guest blog on top sites, and I wanted to keep it at that.

However, I did create three bonus ebooks that you can download completely for free. They each cover one of the two additional key ingredients: creating awesome content, and and finding the time to do it. Below you can learn a little bit more about each ebook and find a link to download one or both of these ebooks completely free.

How to Find Time to Write Great Content

The hardest parts about writing is getting started. In this book, I show you how to overcome writer's block and get in the zone. I'll teach you practical tips that will help you write great content for the rest of your life.

http://mfishbein.com/find-time-write/

Blog Topics That Drive Traffic and Convert Leads

Want free, automated traffic and leads? It's not as difficult as you may think. This book will help you reach massive audiences, build rapport with them, and boost your authority through your blog. And, you won't need to spend lots of money! If you want more traffic and more email subscribers, then this book is for you.

http://mfishbein.com/awesome-content/

More Content Networks

So you've got an awesome product or website...now you just need visitors! Customer acquisition is one of the biggest challenges of building an online business of any kind. This book shows you how to drive traffic to your site using content marketing. You'll learn how to use different platforms to reach new audiences. Give this book a read and get more traffic with content.

http://mfishbein.com/content-marketing-ebook/

Finally, I'd like to thank you for taking the time to read this book. I write books like these in order to can help smart self-learners just like yourself.

I truly hope you found value in this book, and even more, I hope you're able to do something with it.

If you're up for it, I'd really appreciate you leaving me a positive review on Amazon or telling a friend about this book. Your referral is the greatest compliment I can ask for.

www.ingramcontent.com/pod-product-compliance
Lightning Source LLC
Chambersburg PA
CBHW070849180526
45168CB00009B/1109